Improvising w
Mini-Arpeggios

MW00574480

by Paul Musso

To Access the Online Audio Go to:
www.melbay.com/30451BCDEB

Visit us on the Web at www.melbay.com – E-mail us at email@melbay.com

Table of Contents

Improvising with Mini-Arpeggios

One of the most confusing tasks for beginning jazz, blues and rock guitarists is using arpeggios in improvisation. The confusion around how to use arpeggios stems from two sources: learning arpeggios in the two-octave form and understanding arpeggio/scale correlations. This book attempts to solve these problems by introducing Mini-Arpeggios.

Most beginning guitarists learn arpeggios in a two-octave form. These two-octave arpeggios use the sixth and fifth strings as the root notes. The problem with learning these lower-string arpeggios is that there is an inclination to start the arpeggio in the lower octave when improvising. Several times, I recall listening to my students improvise in the mid to upper register using scales and then abruptly jumping down to the sixth string to play an arpeggio. This can sound like a bass line that breaks up the flow of the higher, melodic line. When arpeggios are played in the lower register, it can disrupt the continuity of the melodic line because most musicians improvise in the mid to upper register.

The other problem novice guitarists face is that most of them see scales and arpeggios as very different entities; so much so that they play scales and arpeggios in different places on the neck. There is nothing wrong with learning various arpeggio and scale fingerings. The problem lies in a failure to see the correlation between the scale and arpeggio. When arpeggios and scales are placed in the same position, the guitarist can freely move from one to the other without abrupt changes in musical flow.

This book attempts to alleviate these two common problems guitarists face when trying to improvise with arpeggios by utilizing mini-arpeggios. Mini-arpeggios are one-octave arpeggios, played in the mid to upper register. Mini-arpeggios have root notes on the fourth and third strings; which alleviates the two-octave arpeggio problem. Mini-arpeggios are the upper octave of two-octave arpeggios. The later part of the book illustrates ways to incorporate mini-arpeggios with scales so that the two exist in the same physical space, thus solving the second and more complex problem of moving freely from scales to arpeggios.

The book explores four basic triad arpeggios and five basic seventh chord arpeggios, each set with a fourth string root (Root-4), and a third string root (Root-3). These simple arpeggios are the foundational materials for the entire book. These mini-arpeggios may seem simple and insignificant, but a world of music lies within these simple notes.

The next page illustrates eight basic triad mini-arpeggio shapes. The eight arpeggio fingerings are displayed in tab, notation and chord grid format. Four basic arpeggio types are displayed in both Root-4 and Root-3 classifications: Major, Minor, Diminished and Augmented. Most of the material in this book is based on the **eight-triad mini-arpeggio shapes** on the next page and the **ten seventh chord mini-arpeggios** in chapter one.

Mini-Arpeggios
Basic Triad Shapes

Root-4 (fourth string root)

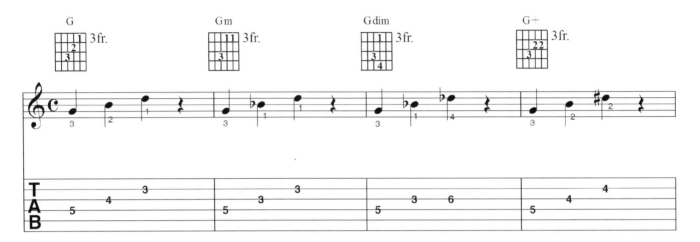

Root-3 (third string root)

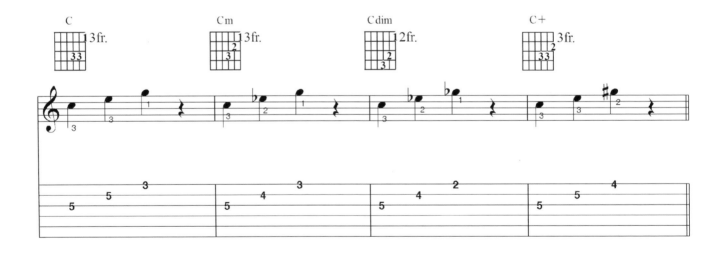

Basic Theory

Triad Arpeggios

The following is a brief explanation of how to create the four basic triad arpeggio types. This explanation is simple and comparative. It is not a substitution for thorough study and analysis of music theory. This explanation involves learning the four arpeggio types by comparing all types to the major arpeggio.

The major arpeggio is derived from the major scale. The following example is a G major scale with each scale degree numbered. "R" represents the root of the scale, chord or arpeggio.

The major arpeggio is derived from the major scale by using the root, 3rd and 5th scale degrees - indicated below by arrows.

When the arrowed chord components are isolated, a G Major arpeggio is created.

G Major arpeggio

The anatomy of the major arpeggio consists of the following intervals: Major 3rd and Perfect 5th (see illustration below). Both intervals are compared to the root note. Comparing each interval to the root note is an excellent way to build the major arpeggio; it insures continuity, rather than building the arpeggio from chord tone to chord tone.

This example is in the key of G Major, but the theory behind creating a major arpeggio is universal to all keys.

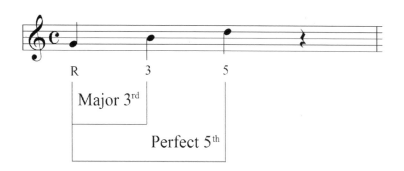

RULE 1: A major arpeggio is constructed by starting on the root of any major scale and then adding the 3rd and 5th. By default, the intervals from the root of a major scale will be: Major 3rd and Perfect 5th.

Now that we have established how to construct a major arpeggio, it is possible to construct the other three arpeggios by altering the major arpeggio. As I said, this is a comparative method and it assumes the proper construction of the major arpeggio.

Lowering the 3rd of the major arpeggio, by a half step, creates a **G minor arpeggio**. The lowered 3rd creates a minor 3rd interval from the root G.

G minor arpeggio

Lowering the 3rd and the 5th of the major arpeggio, by a half step, creates a **G diminished arpeggio**. The lowered 5th creates a diminished 5th interval from the root G.

G diminished arpeggio

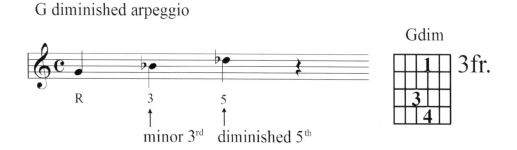

Raising the 5th of the major arpeggio, by a half step, creates a **G Augmented arpeggio**. The raised 5th creates an augmented 5th interval from the root G.

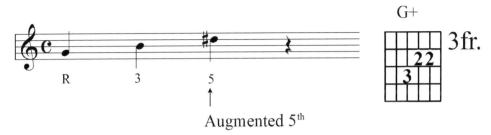

G Augmented arpeggio

G+

R   3   5

Augmented 5th

This graph summarizes how all four basic triad arpeggios are formed.

Triad Construction

Triad Type	Root	3rd	5th
Major	Root	Major 3rd	Perfect 5th
Minor	Root	minor 3rd	Perfect 5th
Diminished	Root	minor 3rd	diminished 5th
Augmented	Root	Major 3rd	Augmented 5th

Seventh Chord Arpeggios

The process of creating seventh chord arpeggios is similar to the process of creating the triad arpeggios in that all arpeggios will use the major seventh arpeggio as a comparative starting point.

Like the major triad, the major seventh arpeggio is derived from the major scale. The following example is a G major scale with each scale degree numbered. "R" represents the root of the scale, chord or arpeggio.

The major seventh arpeggio is derived from the major scale by using the root, 3rd, 5th and 7th scale degrees - indicated below by arrows.

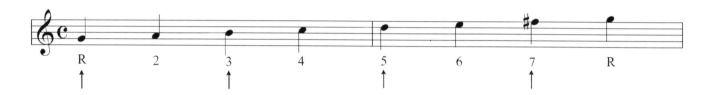

When the arrowed chord components are isolated, a G major seventh arpeggio is created.

Gmaj7

The anatomy of the major seventh arpeggio consists of the following intervals: Major 3rd, Perfect 5th and Major 7th (see illustration below). All three intervals are compared to the root note. Comparing each interval to the root note is a reliable way to build the major seventh arpeggio; it insures continuity, rather than building the arpeggio from chord tone to chord tone.

GMaj7

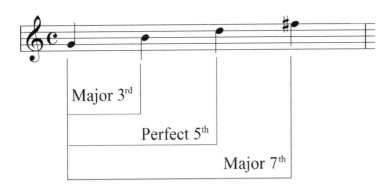

This example is in the key of G major, but the theory behind creating a major seventh arpeggio is universal to all keys.

RULE 2: A major seventh arpeggio is constructed by starting on the root of any major scale and then adding the 3rd, 5th and 7th. By default, the intervals from the root will be: Major 3rd, Perfect 5th and Major 7th.

The four other arpeggio types can be constructed by altering the major seventh arpeggio.

Lowering the seventh scale degree of the major seventh arpeggio, by a half step, creates the dominant seventh arpeggio.

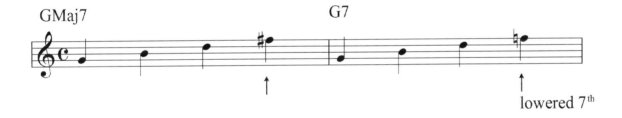

Lowering the major seventh interval by a half step creates a minor seventh interval in this arpeggio. Another way of looking at the construction of the dominant seventh arpeggio is to see it as a major triad with an added minor seventh.

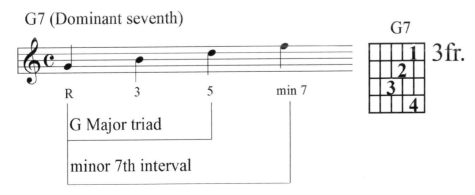

9

The Gm7 arpeggio is created by lowering the 3rd of the G7 arpeggio by a half step. When a major 3rd interval is lowered by a half step, it becomes a minor 3rd interval. This creates a minor triad (G B♭ D). Another way of looking at the construction of the minor seventh arpeggio is to see it as a minor triad with an added minor seventh.

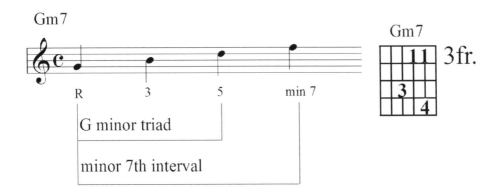

The Gm7(♭5) arpeggio is created by lowering the 5th of the Gm7 arpeggio by a half step. When a Perfect 5th interval is lowered by a half step, it becomes a diminished 5th interval. This creates a diminished triad (G B♭ D♭). Another way of looking at the construction of the minor seventh flat five arpeggio is to see it as a diminished triad with an added minor seventh. The min7(♭5) chord is also called a "half diminished" chord.

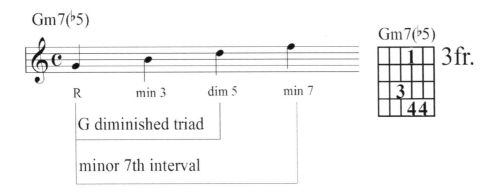

The G diminished seventh arpeggio is created by lowering the 7th of the Gm7(♭5) arpeggio by a half step. When a minor 7th interval is lowered by a half step, it becomes a diminished 7th interval. The diminished 7th interval is the same note as the major 6th interval. In this case, the F♭ (dim7) is the same as E (major 6). Another way of looking at the construction of the diminished seventh arpeggio is to see it as a diminished seventh triad with an added diminished seventh interval.

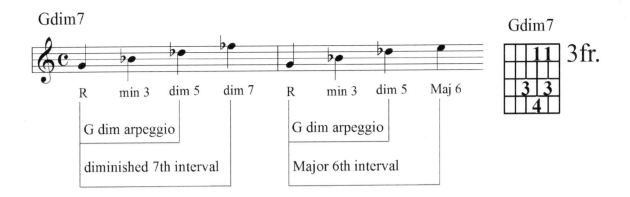

Seventh Chord Construction

Seventh Chord	Triad	7th
Major 7th	Major	Major 7th
Dominant 7th	Major	minor 7th
Minor 7th	minor	minor 7
Minor 7th (♭5)	diminished	minor 7
Diminished 7	diminished	diminished

The following page illustrates these five mini-arpeggios in Root-4 form (Root note on string four) and Root-3 form (Root note on the string three).

Mini-Arpeggios
Seventh Chord
Ten Basic Shapes

Root-4 (fourth string root)

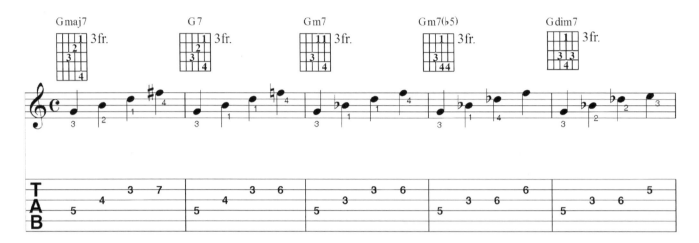

Root-3 (third string root)

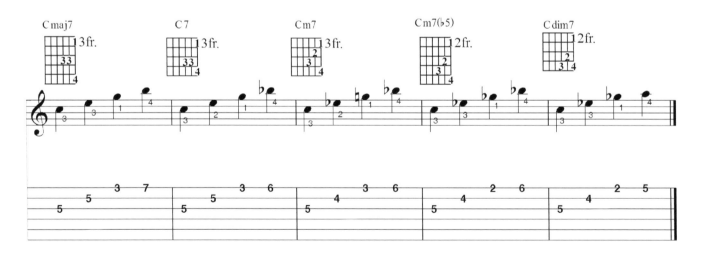

Utilizing Mini-Arpeggios

Note Order

The big question when learning to improvise with arpeggios is: how do I use the arpeggio in an interesting way? Here are three possible approaches on how to use arpeggios to create interesting melodic lines:

Change the note order
Use approach tones
Combine with scales

The first approach is an obvious one: change the note order of the arpeggio. Most musicians practice arpeggios in the order from lowest to highest: Root, 3rd, 5th, and 7th. If we simply start on a different chord tone other than the root, the arpeggio becomes a bit more interesting. The example below uses a G7 arpeggio, starting on the 3rd.

The dominant seventh arpeggio is used in all of the following examples, in order to simplify the concept. Any arpeggio type could be used.

Track 4   (Examples 2, 2.1, 2.2, 2.3)

Ex. 2

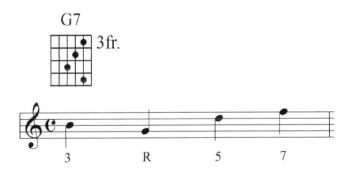

Here are a few more ideas utilizing a rearranged note order with a G7 arpeggio.

Ex. 2.1

There are 24 permutations and combinations for rearranging the four notes of a seventh arpeggio. These combinations are all notated and in tablature from after the first two etudes.

24 Possible Arpeggio Combinations and Permutations:

R 3 5 7	R 3 7 5	R 5 3 7	R 5 7 3	R 7 3 5	R 7 5 3
3 R 5 7	3 R 7 5	3 5 R 7	3 5 7 R	3 7 R 5	3 7 5 R
5 R 3 7	5 R 7 3	5 3 R 7	5 3 7 R	5 7 R 3	5 7 3 R
7 R 3 5	7 R 5 3	7 3 R 5	7 3 5 R	7 5 R 3	7 5 3 R

Here is an interesting little lick based on the 7 3 5 R sequence. Notice how simple this melody is. It contains notes from the arpeggio and nothing more. I've only added a simple rhythmic figure to make it more interesting.

Ex. 2.2

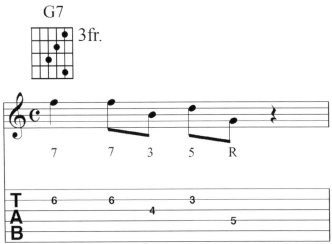

This motif could be a springboard for another melodic idea. If this were a blues progression, I could refer to the melodic contour (7 3 5 R) on the next chord – C7.

Ex. 2.3

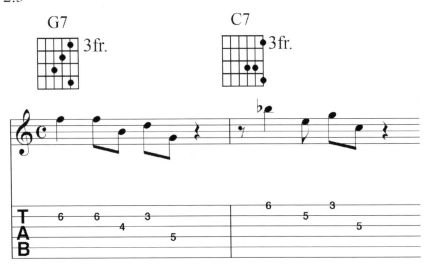

The etude on the following page utilizes five different mini-arpeggios in a G jazz blues progression. I primarily use chord tones, but the melody is effective and memorable. I only added a few chromatic notes for color. The (7 3 5 R) sequence is the basis for this etude.

Mini-Arpeggio Etude 1

Paul Musso

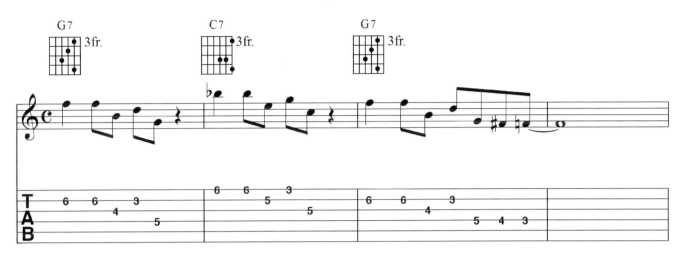

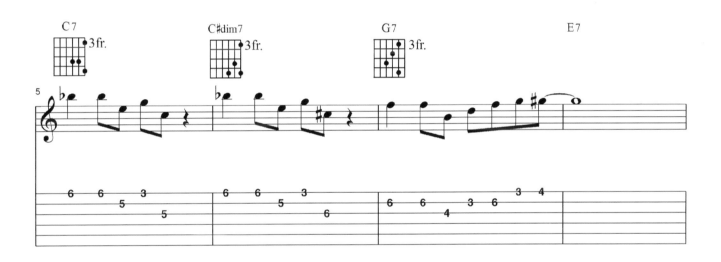

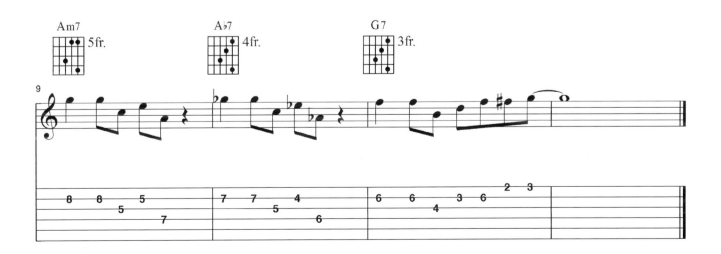

Track 6

Mini-Arpeggio Etude 2

This etude utilizes mini-arpeggios with
different note order sequences.

Paul Musso

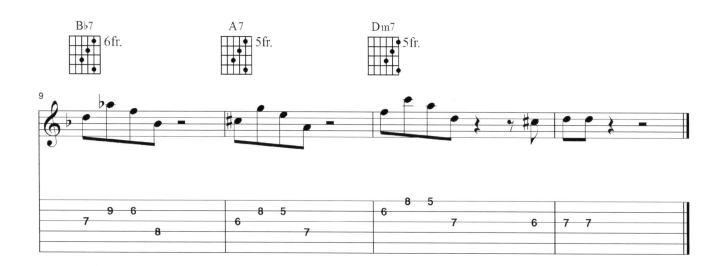

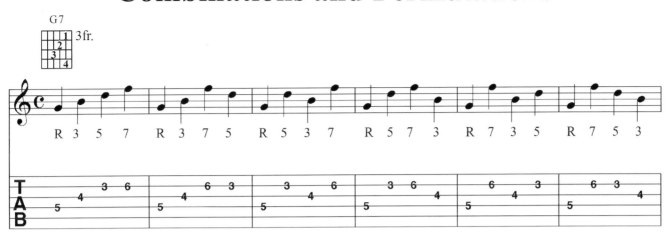

24 Arpeggio
Combinations and Permutations

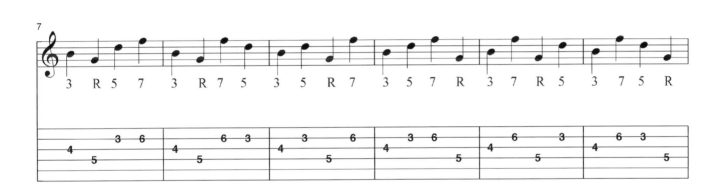

This page has been left blank to avoid awkward page turns.

Approach Tones

Approach Tones From Below

The second technique in making arpeggios interesting is utilizing approach tones. Approach tones are notes that are either a whole step or a half step above or below the chord tone.

Four Possible Approach Tones

Half Step Below	Half Step Above
Whole Step Below	Whole Step above

Here is an example of the G7 mini-arpeggio with half-step-below approach tones on every chord tone. *Notice the left hand suggested finger numbers.*

Track 8   (Examples 3, 3.1, 3.2, 3.3)

Ex. 3

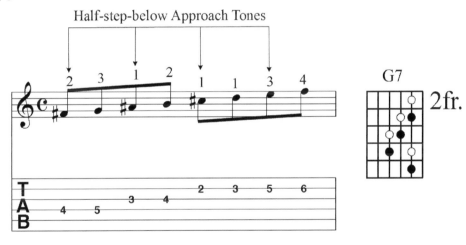

If I simply use one half-step-below approach tone, I can create an effective melodic idea. The following G7 lick uses a Bb, which is the approach tone below the major third-B.

Ex. 3.1   Half Step Below Approach Tone

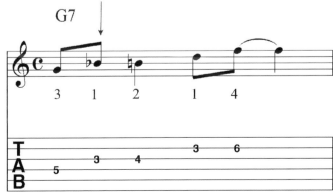

This next lick is a Django-style lick that could be used over a dominant chord or a major chord. The idea is based on a descending major arpeggio without a seventh. The line utilizes a half-step-below approach concept. Holding true to Django, I used only the first two fingers of the left hand.

Ex. 3.2

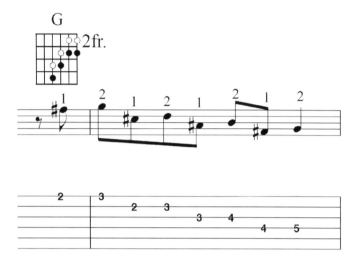

I can now take my (7 3 5 R) idea from the previous section and add a single approach tone to each arpeggio. At this point, this line begins to sound more sophisticated and more stylistically like a jazz idea.

The approach tones create an effective and logical use of chromaticism (consecutive half steps) within the context of playing chord tones from the arpeggio.

Ex. 3.3

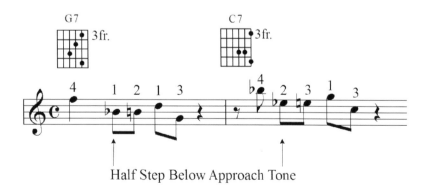

Half Step Below Approach Tone

The next etude is based on Etude 1, but utilizes half step-below approach tones on the 3rd of each chord.

Mini-Arpeggio Etude 3

Paul Musso

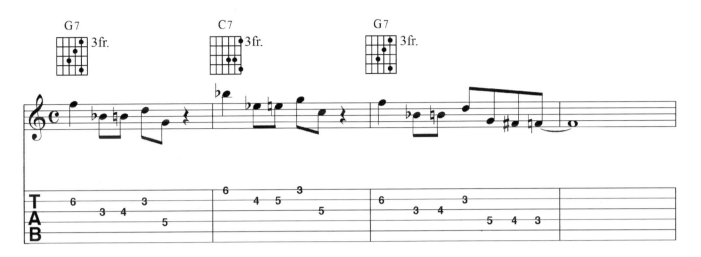

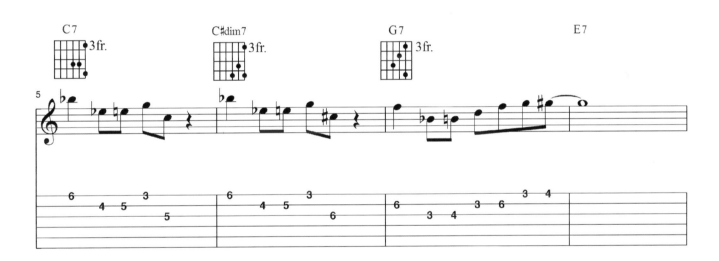

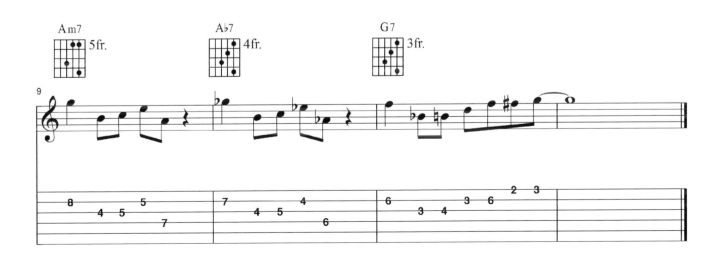

Approach Tones From Above – Chromatic

The next step is to examine approach tones from above. One of the simplest melodic devices is using half steps above each chord tone.

Here is the same G triad that I used in the last section with half step approach tones from above rather than half step approach tones from below. I only used the first and second fingers of the left hand for this melody; feel free to use any finger combination that feels more comfortable.

Track 10   (Examples 3.4, 3.5, 3.6, 3.7, 3.8, 3.9, 3.9.1, 3.9.2, 3.9.3)

Ex. 3.4

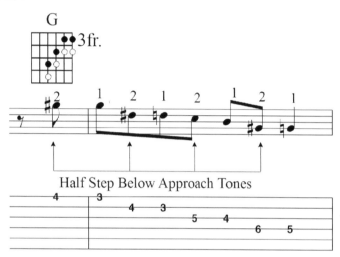

Half Step Below Approach Tones

Notice how "exotic" this melody sounds. This is because the melody is reminiscent of the Phrygian mode. The Phrygian mode is sometimes used to improvise over a chord progression of two major triads that are one half step apart – G G#. The Phrygian mode is also used over iii minor chords and altered dominant seventh chords. The last part of this book covers scale theory in depth, so don't be concerned if the concept isn't entirely clear at this time. The lick above contains both triads. It also contains the five of the seven notes in a G Phrygian scale:

G Phrygian: G A♭ B♭ C D E♭ F
G Triad lick: G (G#)   C D (D#)

You may find this sound a bit too "altered" if you were playing over a G6 or GMaj7, however; this lick would be fitting if the chord was G7#5 or G7♭9. The A♭ and D# would be effective note choices in this "altered-dominant" application.

Because of this altered sound, many improvisers prefer to use diatonic steps from above.

Approach Tones From Above - Diatonic

This next example uses diatonic steps from above: A precedes G, E precedes D and C precedes B. All of the approach tones are diatonic or "in the key of" G. This sound is more consonant and thus, is conducive to playing over the G chord as a I chord (GMaj7, G6) or over a G7 in a blues context.

Ex. 3.5

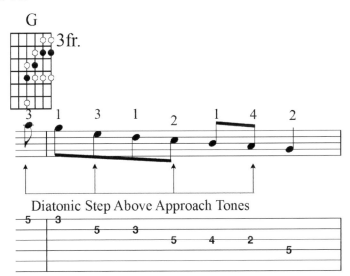

Diatonic Step Above Approach Tones

One commonly used device when expanding the use of the mini-arpeggio in the triad setting is to play the diatonic whole step above and the chromatic half step below (example below). Notice how sophisticated this melody starts to sound. The technique is simply surrounding the triad by whole steps above and half steps below.

Ex. 3.6

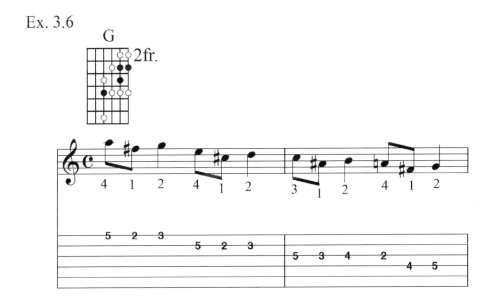

In the first section, I talked about changing the note order so that the arpeggio isn't always played Root 3rd 5th. If I apply that rule to this lick, I could come up with some very interesting melodic ideas. This example moves in fifths by following the chord tone order: Root 5th 3rd.

Ex. 3.7

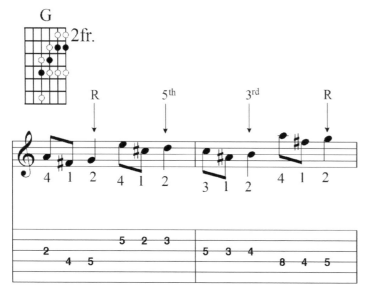

Now it's time to put these upper approach tones into some jazz motifs that incorporate the seventh chord mini-arpeggio. The following lick is based on one of the examples from the last section.

Ex. 3.8

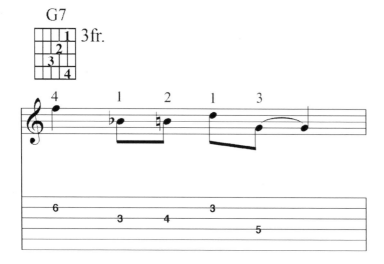

I can add a diatonic approach tone above one note in this lick to make it a little more intricate and more stylistically jazz-sounding. The pickup note G is a diatonic step above the chord tone F.

Ex. 3.9

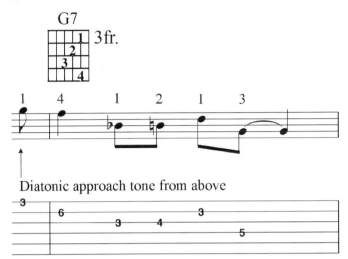

I will now apply these upper approach tones to the first two bars of a G blues progression. Notice how the same melodic contour is applied to both the G7 and C7 arpeggios, creating melodic continuity. The first example uses diatonic steps from above.

Ex. 3.9.1

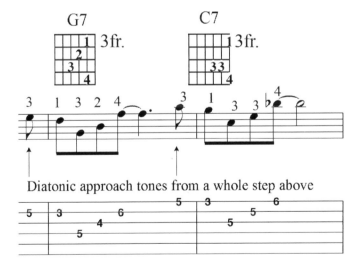

If I use chromatic, half-step-from-above approach tones on this same example, the line becomes more altered and exotic.

Ex. 3.9.2

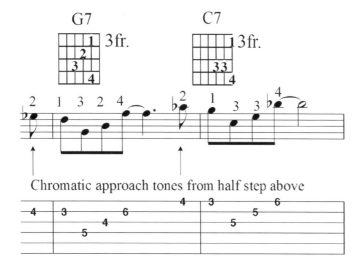

Chromatic approach tones from half step above

Combining Chromatic and Diatonic

This next example uses several different approach tone concepts to create a motif for the first two bars of a G blues progression. This line uses a half step below idea (Bb –B) as well as two diatonic approach tones from above (E-D and A-G). Notice also how the second bar, played over C7, is not an exact copy of the first bar when it comes to intervals and melodic contour. The second bar hints at the first bar as a logical answer to the question posed by the first bar, like a call and response.

Ex. 3.9.3

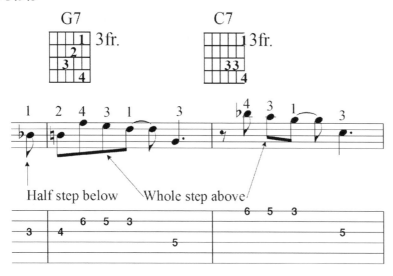

Half step below   Whole step above

Combining all approach tone types to the mini- arpeggio can create endless melodic ideas that disguise the simplicity of the core concept - **the arpeggio**.

The next etude uses half-step approach tones from above and focuses on the 5th and 7th of the chord. It is also based on a G blues progression.

Mini-Arpeggio Etude 4

Paul Musso

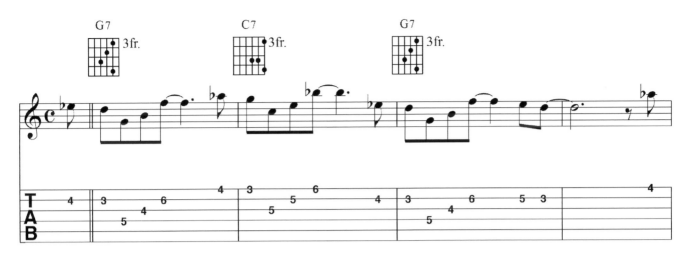

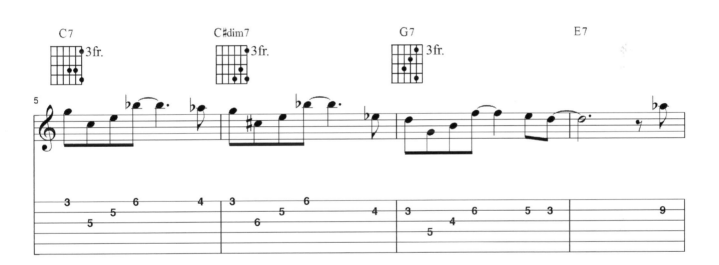

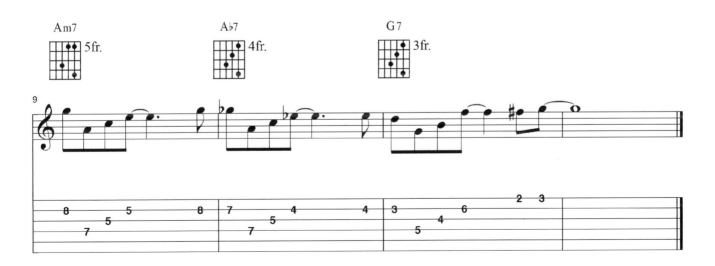

The following six pages contain a series of mini-arpeggio licks that can be used for major, minor and dominant chords.

Mini-Arpeggio
Major Licks
Root - 4

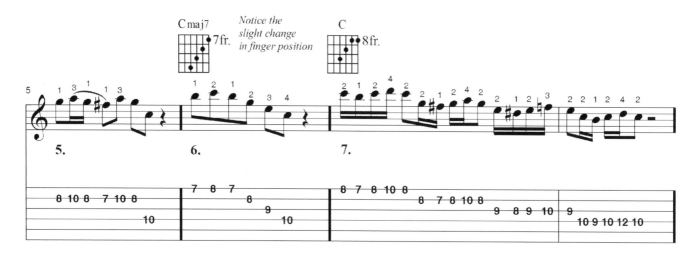

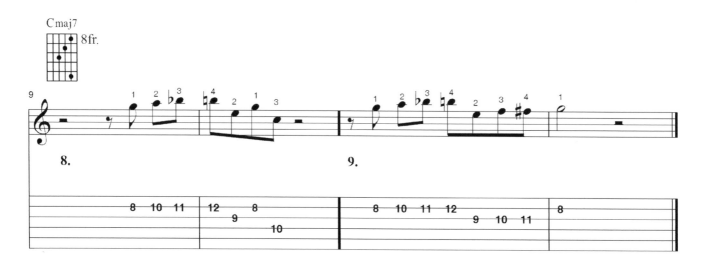

28

Mini-Arpeggio
Major Licks
Root - 3

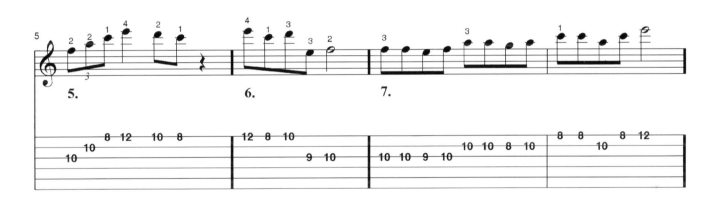

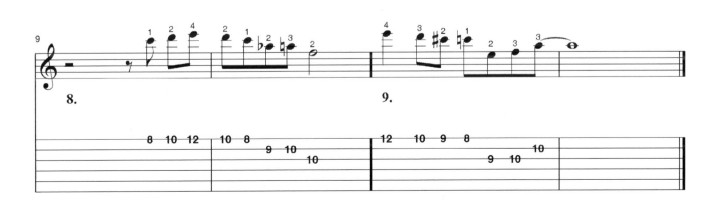

Mini-Arpeggio
Minor Licks
Root - 4

30

Mini-Arpeggio
Minor Licks
Root - 3

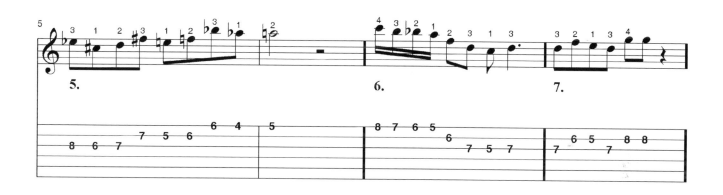

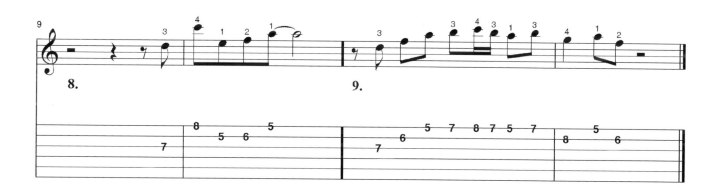

Mini-Arpeggio
Dominant Seventh Licks
Root - 4

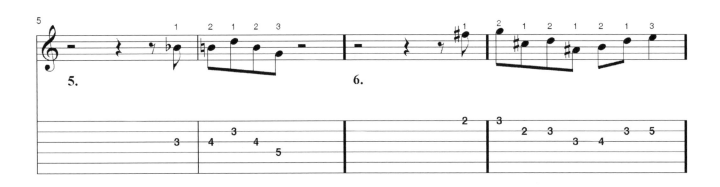

Mini-Arpeggio
Dominant Seventh Licks
Root - 3

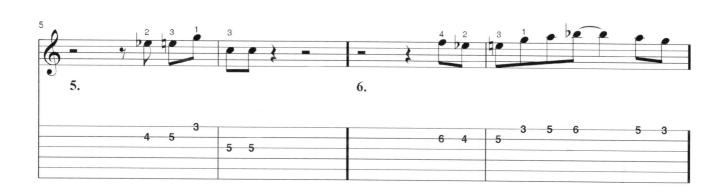

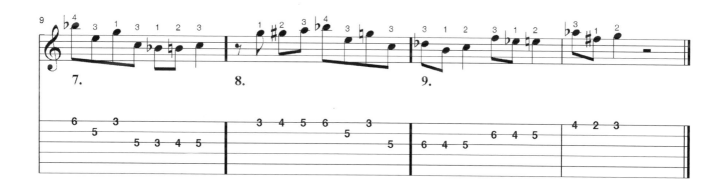

33

This page has been left blank to avoid awkward page turns.

Improvising Over ii V I Progressions

The licks from the previous section focus on isolated single chords and can be used in a variety of contexts. The next step is to look at utilizing mini-arpeggios in improvisation over the ii V I progression, which is one of the most commonly used progressions in jazz and popular music. The ii V I progression was even used by composers as far back as Bach. The ability to play over ii V I progressions intelligently and skillfully is the beginning of what jazz players have dubbed "playing over the changes." Mini-arpeggios make it possible to address complex chord progressions because of their simple structure.

There are two basic patterns that occur when using mini-arpeggios over the ii V I progression: (Root-4 Root-3 Root-4) and (Root-3 Root-4 Root-3).

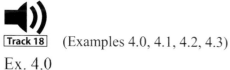

Track 18   (Examples 4.0, 4.1, 4.2, 4.3)

Ex. 4.0

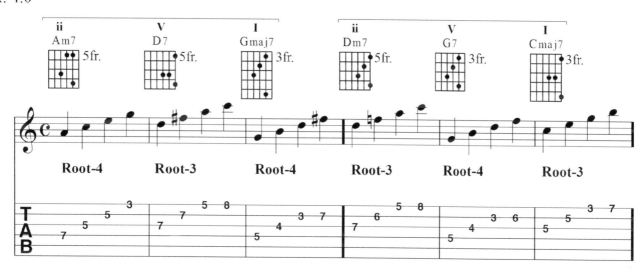

These patterns coincide with the same fret numbers as the chords commonly played in these two ii V I progressions. Root-4 mini-arpeggios are always in the same position as Root-6 barre chords. Root-3 mini-arpeggios are always in the same position as Root-5 barre chords.

	ii	V	I
ARPEGGIO	Root-4	Root-3	Root-4
CHORD	Root-6	Root-5	Root-6
	same position	same position	same position

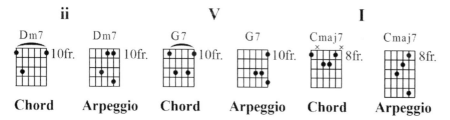

	ii	V	I
ARPEGGIO	Root-3	Root-4	Root-3
CHORD	Root-5	Root-6	Root-5
	same position	same position	same position

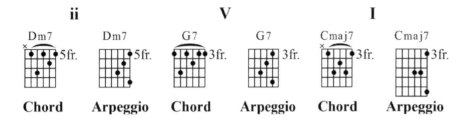

Another advantage of these mini-arpeggio fingerings is that they are completely in sync with the chord knowledge skill set that most novice guitarists already know. The simple Root-6 and Root-5 barre chords and power chords are easy to locate on the fretboard, making mini-arpeggios just as easy to find.

Improvising over these progressions in a musical way involves a bit of forethought. The first step is to incorporate a few approach tones on the note before the chord change occurs. In the following example, the approach tones occur on beat four. The C♯ is a half-step-below approach tone and the G♯ is a half-step-above approach tone.

Ex. 4.1

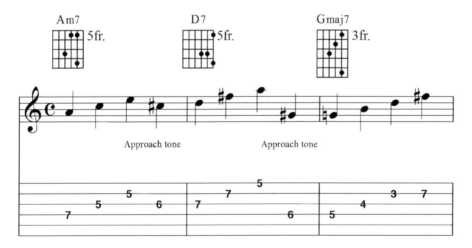

If we add a few simple rhythms to the idea above, the example becomes more musical and inventive. The example below makes much more of a musical statement and becomes a legitimate ii V I lick. Notice how I didn't add a single note beyond the arpeggio tones.

Ex. 4.2

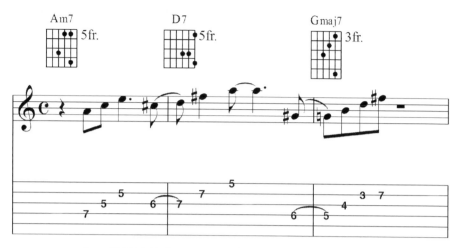

When constructing ii V I licks, remember to target chord tones on the beat where the chord change occurs. Eventually this rule can be broken, but keep it in mind as you are starting the process of playing over chord changes.

The next example uses the same arpeggios as the two previous examples, but the chord changes occur in half the time. This is known as a one bar ii V because the ii and V chords occupy one measure. Notice how the approach tones occur before the chord changes and how the chord tones occur on the beat when the chord change takes place.

Ex. 4.3

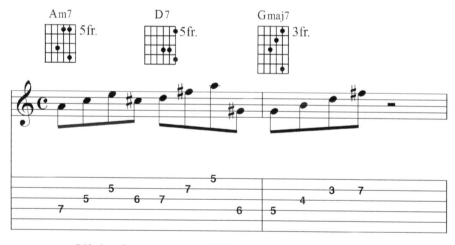

The next set of licks focuses on ii V I progressions. Some of the licks are over two bar ii V progressions and some are over one bar ii V progressions. The licks incorporate many of the devices mentioned in previous sections of this book, specifically note order combinations and various approach tones. Some additional tones, outside of the arpeggio and approach tones, may appear. These additional notes are covered in the last section of this book under Combining Mini-Arpeggios With Scales.

It is essential for every improvising jazz musician to have a vocabulary consisting of various ii V I licks. These licks are a part of the language of improvisation, similar to learning sentences in a foreign language. Eventually these licks, like sentences, can be strung together to form complete solos, like paragraphs.

ii VI Licks
Starting on Root - 4

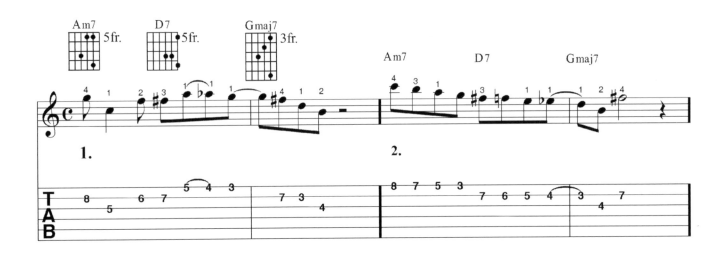

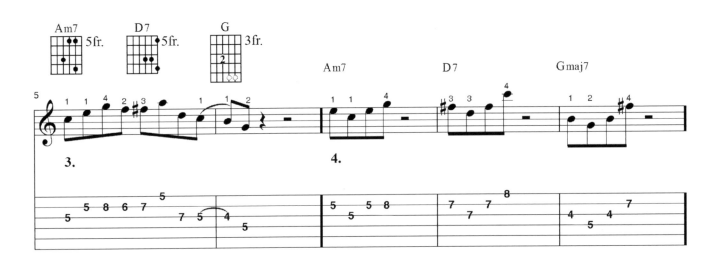

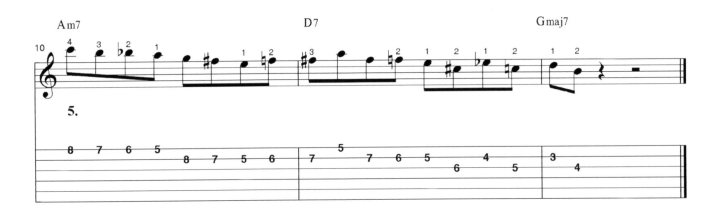

ii VI Licks
Starting on Root - 3

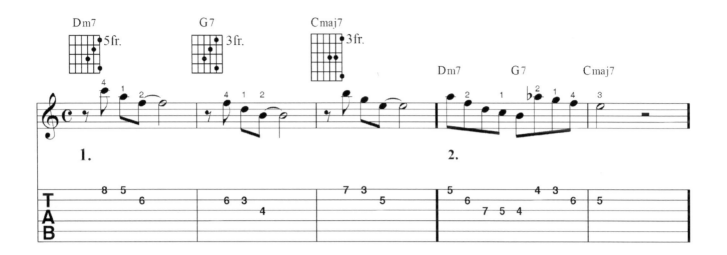

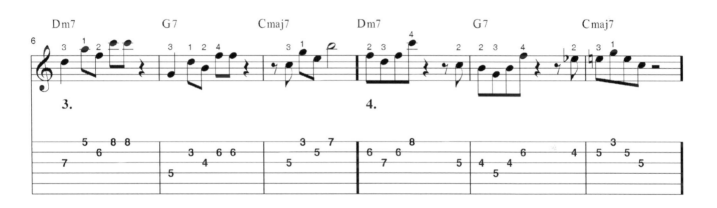

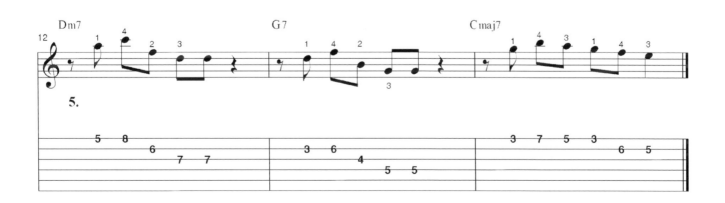

This etude incorporates mini-arpeggio ii V I ideas in various keys.

ii V I
Circle Etude

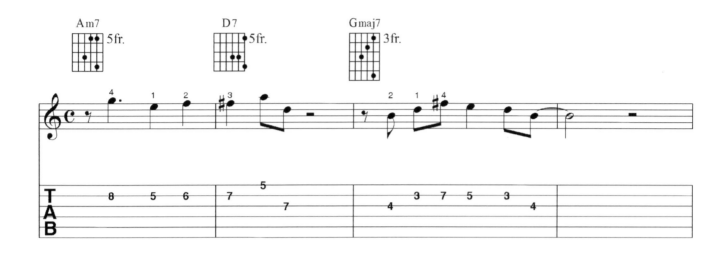

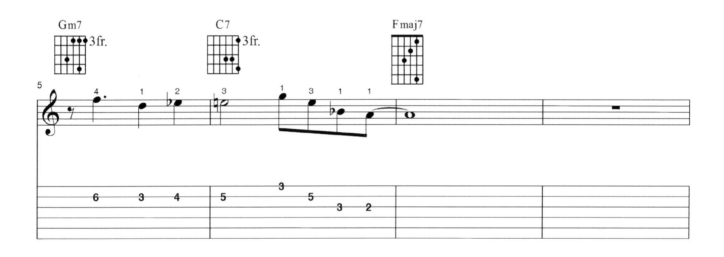

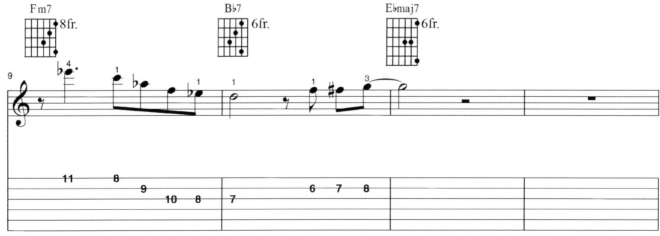

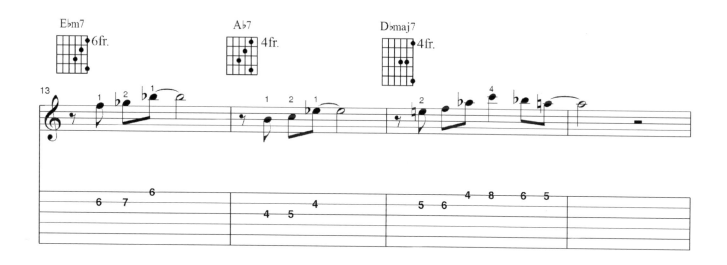

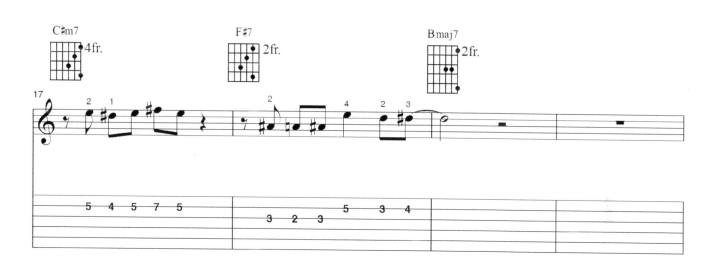

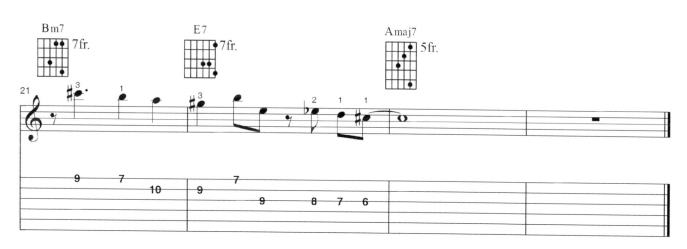

This page has been left blank to avoid awkward page turns.

Combining Mini-Arpeggios With Scales

Dominant Seventh: Mixolydian and Blues

The next step is to examine how to use the mini-arpeggio in tandem with scales.

Improvising should be a seamless combination of scales and chords. Most novice guitarists don't see the relationship of the scale to the arpeggio and play scales in different positions than arpeggios. Good improvisers have a solid grasp of both arpeggios and scales and they see both as one entity. It is imperative to see the symbiotic relationship between the scale and the arpeggio. Scales and arpeggios must be played and conceptualized in the same area of the fretboard in order for this relationship to exist.

The following example illustrates a G Mixolydian scale, in the third position, followed by a G7 mini-arpeggio in the third position. Notice how the G7 arpeggio is hidden within the G Mixolydian scale.

Track 22 (Examples 5.0, 5.1, 5.2, 5.3, 5.4, 5.5, 5.6, 5.7, 5.8, 5.9, 5.9.1, 5.9.2, 5.9.3, 5.9.4, 5.9.5, 5.9.6, 5.9.7, 5.9.8, 5.9.9, 6.0, 6.1)

Ex. 5.0

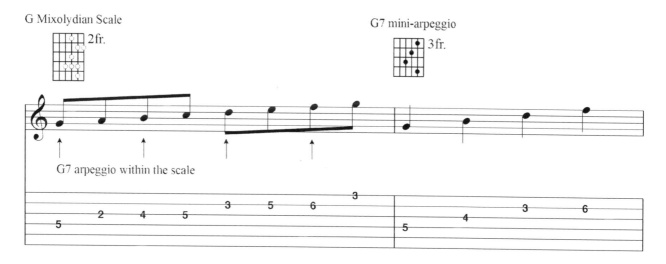

When these two concepts are combined, the scale and arpeggio become one entity. The arpeggio notes (in black) are highlighted (below). The arpeggio is highlighted because the chord tones have more emphasis; they are "magnetized" in a sense. This graphic is exactly how one should visualize the fretboard when a mini-arpeggio is combined with a scale.

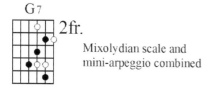

Mixolydian scale and
mini-arpeggio combined

Here is a bebop lick using G Mixolydian emphasizing the G7 chord tones. Notice how many chord tones are utilized. This is what I mean by magnetizing the arpeggio.

Ex. 5.1

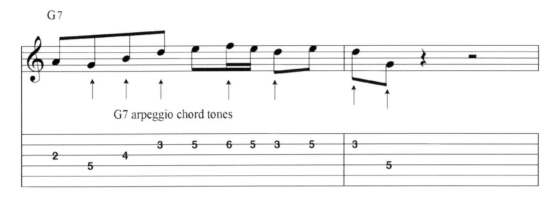

This next lick utilizes a device commonly used by swing musicians like Lester Young and Charlie Christian. Often, a soloist would play the arpeggio ascending and then descend with the scale.

Ex. 5.2

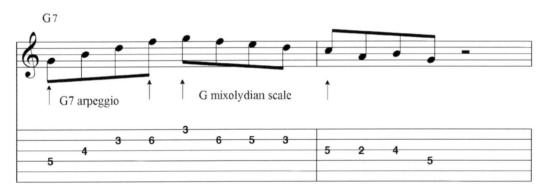

The next step is combining the G7 arpeggio with a blues scale in the same position. The blues scale contains the chord tones B♭ (♭3) and D♭ (♭5). These notes are not in the G7 arpeggio, so the combined scale becomes an entirely new sound with a string of four chromatic notes: B♭ B C D♭ D.

Ex. 5.3

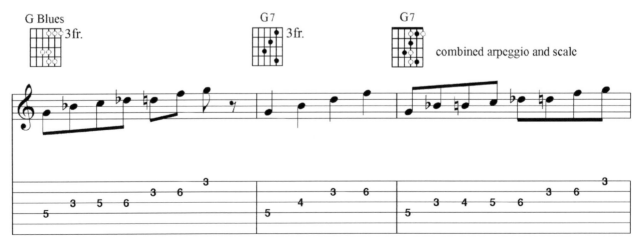

Here is a melodic idea that incorporates the combination of a G blues scale and a G7 mini-arpeggio.

Ex. 5.4

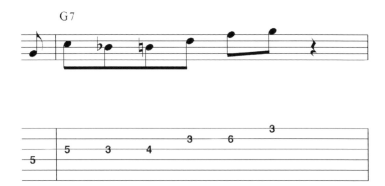

This next idea combines both the arpeggio and scale, ascending with a G7 arpeggio and descending with a G blues scale.

Ex. 5.5

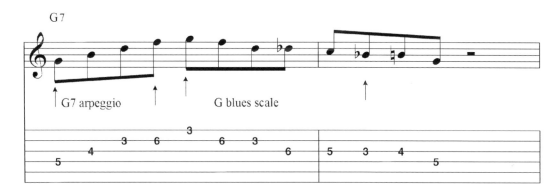

Notice how the previous licks all revolve around the basic arpeggio yet still sound interesting. Don't think that emphasizing the arpeggio is in any way a "beginner" technique. The arpeggio is one of the most important and useful tools when improvising – never underestimate this concept.

Minor Modes: Dorian, Aeolian and Phrygian

The three minor modes that contain a minor seventh chord are: Dorian, Aeolian and Phrygian. The Dorian mode contains a major 2nd and major 6th. The Aeolian mode contains a major 2nd and a minor 6th. The Phrygian mode contains a minor 2nd and a minor 6th. These seconds and sixths help to define each mode.

Here is a Gm7 arpeggio followed by a G Dorian mode. Notice the arpeggio notes in black embedded within the G Dorian scale.

Ex. 5.6

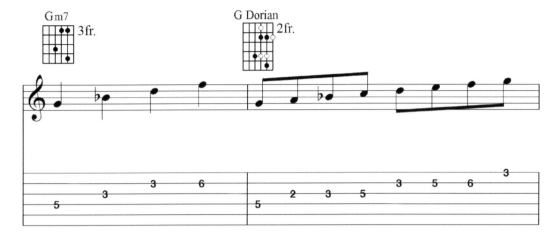

The following lick combines the Gm7 arpeggio as well as the major 6th note E. The major 6th clearly defines the melody as a Dorian sound.

Ex. 5.7

Here is a Gm7 arpeggio followed by a G Aeolian mode. Notice how the two are in the same position. The only difference between the Aeolian mode and the Dorian mode is that the Aeolian mode has a minor 6th. It is helpful to think of the Aeolian mode as the Dorian mode with a flat 6th. Notice the arpeggio notes in black, within the G Aeolian mode.

Ex. 5.8

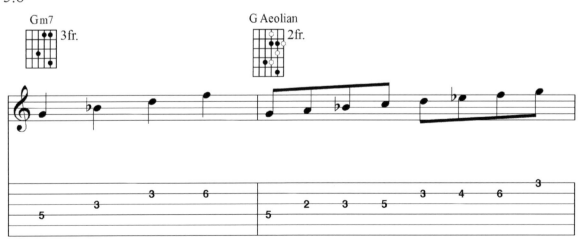

This G Aeolian lick uses the minor 6th along with chord tones. The minor 6th (E♭) defines the melody as Aeolian.

Ex. 5.9

Here is a Gm7 arpeggio followed by a G Phrygian mode. The Phrygian mode is like the Aeolian mode with a flat 2nd (minor 2nd). Notice the arpeggio notes in black, within the G Phrygian mode.

Ex. 5.9.1

This melody defines the Phrygian mode by using both the minor 2nd (A♭) and the minor 6th (E♭). Notice how the chord tones occur on the strong beats.

Ex. 5.9.2

This table summarizes the differences between the three minor Greek modes.

Scale Degrees	1	2	3	4	5	6	7
Dorian	Root	Maj 2nd	min 3rd	Perfect 4	Perfect 5th	Maj 6th	min 7th
Aeolian	Root	Maj 2nd	min 3rd	Perfect 4	Perfect 5th	min 6th	min 7th
Phrygian	Root	min 2nd	min 3rd	Perfect 4	Perfect 5th	min 6th	min 7th

Major Modes: Ionian and Lydian

The following example illustrates a G major scale, in the third position, followed by a GMaj7 mini-arpeggio in the third position. Notice how the GMaj7 is a part of the G major scale.

Ex. 5.9.3

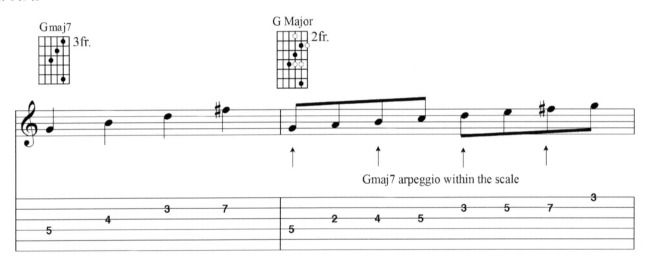

Once again, I need to emphasize that the notes in the arpeggio are "magnetized". Your fingers and ears should become drawn to chord tones in the arpeggio while improvising.

The next lick is a simple G major idea. Notice that five chord tones are used from the mini-arpeggio.

Ex. 5.9.4

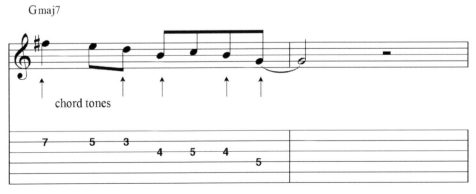

The following idea is another G major melody that incorporates the GMaj7 mini-arpeggio and the G major scale. It also uses a bit of chromaticism (E F F♯). Notice how most of the chord tones (G B D F♯) are played on strong beats.

Ex. 5.9.5

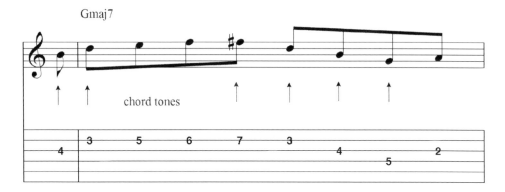

The other scale used in conjunction with the major seventh chord is the Lydian mode. The Lydian mode features the sharp fourth scale degree (C♯ in the key of G). This mode is considered to be the "brightest" sounding scale due to the raised fourth scale degree.

The fingering of this scale may seem a bit strange due to the four notes on the B string (C♯ D E F♯). This is because of the F♯ on the second string. The second example incorporates an alternate finger pattern that may be more intuitive, logical and easier to play.

Ex. 5.9.6

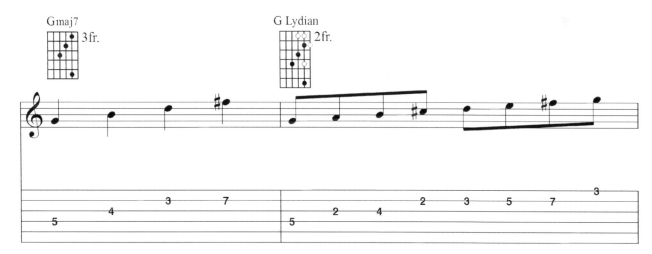

Alternate Finger Pattern

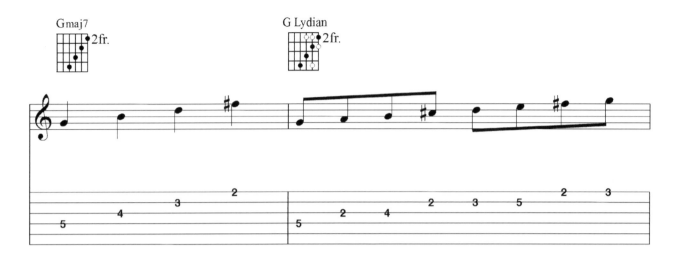

Modal licks and melodies must contain the specific notes that make the mode unique. In this case, the sharp four (C♯) needs to be incorporated into the lick. If the sharp four is placed on a strong beat (1234), it has even more of an impact. The following short melody uses the C♯ on beat one, which defines a Lydian sound.

The following example demonstrates two different ways to play this lick. The first fingering uses the GMaj7 mini-arpeggio fingering with the F♯ on the first string. The second GMaj7 fingering uses the original mini-arpeggio, root-four fingering with the F♯ on the second string. Both arpeggio fingerings are valid; each fingering accommodates different licks.

Ex. 5.9.7

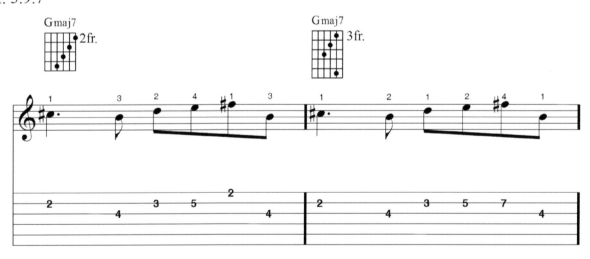

Locrian Mode

The Locrian mode is used, almost exclusively, to improvise over minor seventh flat five chords. Here is the arpeggio/scale pattern for Gm7(♭5). Notice how easy the fingering is for the G Locrian mode. This is due to the parent key, A♭ major. This major scale finger pattern is very common to all guitarists. The Locrian mode pattern ends up feeling very natural.

Ex. 5.9.8

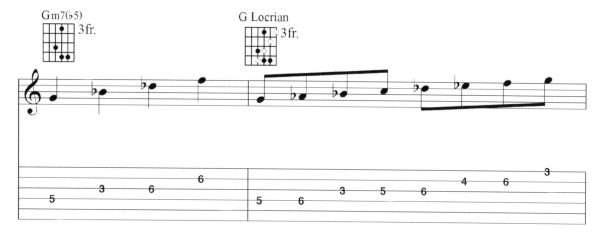

The harmonic context for a minor seventh flat five chord is usually a ii chord in the minor key. Most of the time, the m7(♭5) is followed by a V chord in minor. This means that the Gm7(♭5) is a ii chord in F minor and the V chord is C7. The following lick demonstrates a ii V lick in F minor. Notice how the lick starts on the third of Gm7(♭5) - B♭ and lands on the third of C7 – E. Targeting chord tones on downbeats is an excellent way to define the harmonic progression. This is what is commonly called "making the changes" because the melodic material can stand on its own without being dependent on the presence of the chord changes.

Ex. 5.9.9

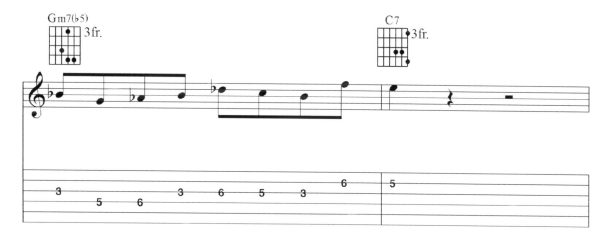

Phrygian Mode as an Altered Scale

The Phrygian mode can be used as an altered scale. Teachers, when explaining mode applications, often overlook this concept. The Phrygian mode is usually played over minor chords, but it can also be played over altered dominant chords like G7(♯5♭9). Using the Phrygian mode as an altered dominant scale is an easy way to add altered tones to basic arpeggios. When the Phrygian mode is played over a dominant seventh chord, the following altered notes are present: ♭9, ♯9 and ♯5. The Phrygian mode can be used over dominant seventh chords, even though the mode is missing the third of the dominant seventh chord.

This page has been left blank to avoid awkward page turns.

The following graphic illustrates the combination of the G7 mini-arpeggio and the G Phrygian scale. The result creates a G Spanish Phrygian scale. The Spanish Phrygian scale is a Phrygian scale with an added major third. The only note from the G7 arpeggio that is not in the G Phrygian scale is the B natural. The B♭ is not seen as a ♭3, but rather a ♯9. This scale is excellent for improvising over dominant seventh chords that resolve – G7 to Cmaj7 or G7 to Cm7.

Ex. 6.0

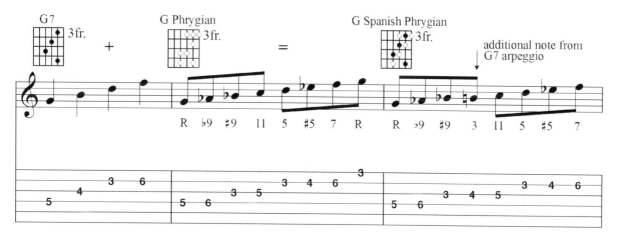

The following lick incorporates elements of this unique arpeggio/scale combination. Notice how I used all of the altered notes in the Phrygian scale: ♭9, ♯9, and ♯5. I also target the major 3rd (E) of the CMaj7 chord. The Phrygian scale creates a "darker" color for the G7 chord. When the CMaj7 is played, it sounds "bright" in contrast to the preceding Phrygian scale.

Ex. 6.1

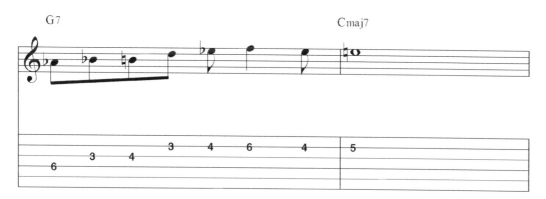

This section used the Root-4 arpeggio as a model for arpeggio/scale combinations. The next section summarizes Root-3 and Root-4 arpeggios combined with scales and modes.

Arpeggio/Scale Combinations
Root-3

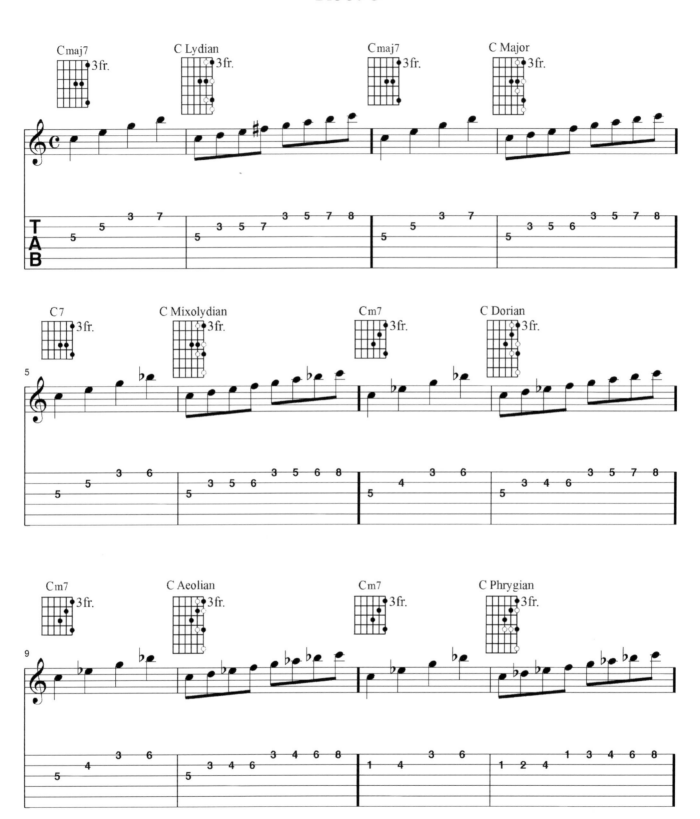

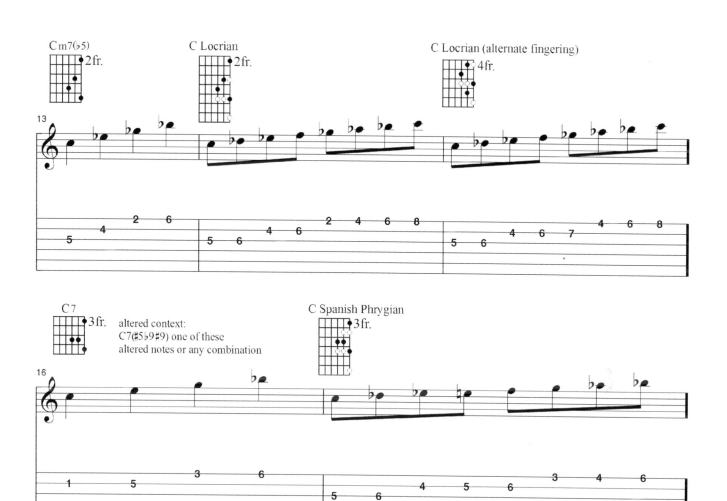

Arpeggio/Scale Combinations
Root-4

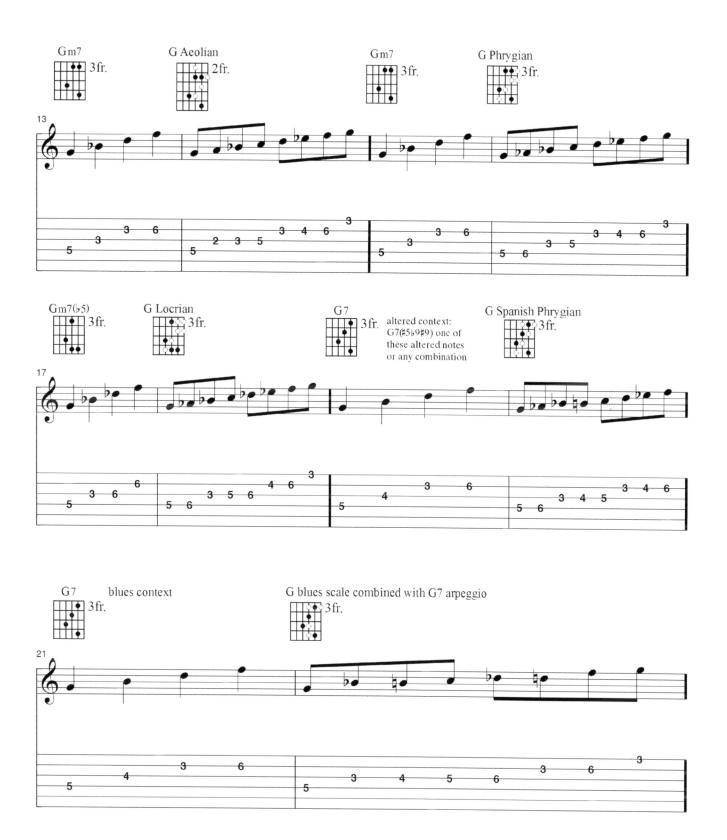

This page has been left blank to avoid awkward page turns.

Ultimate Mini-Arpeggio Challenge

The chart below consists of random arpeggios with no harmonic relationship to each other. The ultimate challenge is to play this chart without stopping. Try the following approaches in the execution of this chart:

1. Play all as Root-4 mini-arpeggios (free rhythm)

2. Play all as Root-3 mini-arpeggios (free rhythm)

Track 25

3. Play all as Root-4 mini-arpeggios (in time – quarter notes – 50 beats per measure) Audio Example

Track 26

4. Play all as Root-3 mini-arpeggios (in time – quarter notes – 50 beats per measure) Audio Example

Track 27

5. Play the chart utilizing the least amount of movement from arpeggio to arpeggio – 100 beats per measure Audio Example

Dm7	F7	E♭Maj7	Am7(♭5)
GMaj7	Em7	Cdim7	B7
Ddim7	Gm7	C#7	E♭7
A7	DMaj7	B♭m7	EMaj7
F#m7	Cm7	G7	Edim7
FMaj7	Am7	A♭Maj7	D7
CMaj7	Gm7(♭5)	D♭Maj7	Fm7(♭5)
Dm7(♭5)	B♭Maj7	Cm7(♭5)	Gdim7
E♭m7	F#Maj7	AMaj7	Em7(♭5)
A♭7	Fm7	G#7	Bm7
F#7	C7	A♭dim7	B♭7

Author's Notes

I hope this book on mini-arpeggios has been helpful in your pursuit to master guitar improvisation. I have covered a large amount of information throughout this book and I encourage you to practice and process this information methodically and slowly. I have used these principles over the last twenty years and I assure you that your improvisation skills will improve if you incorporate these concepts and techniques.

Paul Musso

About the Author

Paul Musso is an Assistant Professor and Area Head of Music Performance in the Music and Entertainment Industry Studies Department at the University of Colorado Denver. Paul has been with UC Denver for twenty five years teaching fretboard harmony, fretboard melody, commercial guitar styles, applied guitar studies, jazz theory, songwriting, improvisation and guitar ensembles. He is the author of three Mel Bay publications for jazz guitar: Fingerstyle Jazz Guitar/Teaching Your Guitar to Walk, Graded Fingerstyle Jazz Guitar Solos and Fingerstyle Jazz Guitar Chord Soloing. Paul is a co-author of Mel Bay's 2000 Jazz Guitar, where Paul shares the bill with greats Johnny Smith, John Abercrombie, Buckey Pizzarelli, George Van Eps, Andy Summers and many others. Paul is a freelance guitarist and has performed throughout the Colorado area with many diverse ensembles including the Colorado Symphony, the Boulder Festival Orchestra, the Aspen Music Festival, and the Westcliff Jazz Festival. Paul has also performed throughout Europe, Mexico and the United States. His recent critically acclaimed CD Tonescapes is available for download on iTunes.

"Tonescapes is a beautiful CD with great tone and melodic surprises." - Jim Hall

"Musso dotes on each and every note, listening to them swing and ring." - Marc Myers, JazzWax.Com

Made in the USA
San Bernardino, CA
29 April 2018